SAMPLE JOKES

Why did the goldfish think they were fighting a battle? **They were inside a tank.**

How do you throw birthday party in outer space? **You planet.**

Why don't they don't allow gambling during a safari? **Too many Cheetahs.**

What do you call a horse that lives in the house next to you?
A neeeeeeigh-bor.

Why don't vampires eat meat? **They don't like steaks.**

1

BONUS! Keep track of your score!

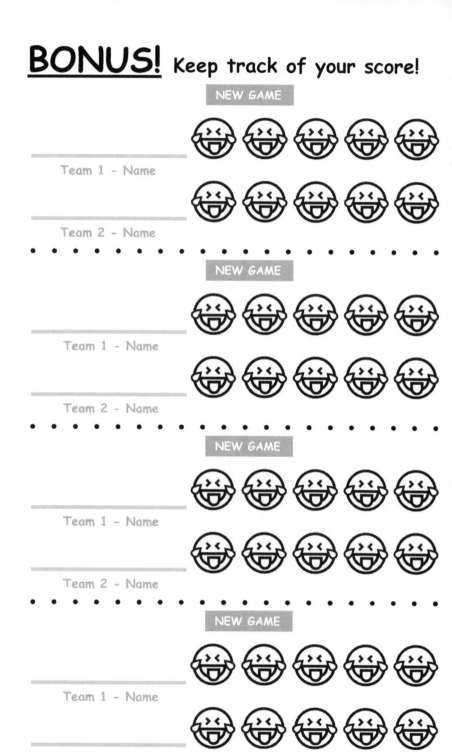

NEW GAME

Team 1 - Name

Team 2 - Name

NEW GAME

Team 1 - Name

Team 2 - Name

NEW GAME

Team 1 - Name

Team 2 - Name

NEW GAME

Team 1 - Name

Team 2 - Name

TRY NOT TO LAUGH OUT LOUD CHALLENGE

INCLUDES SCORE PAGES!

JOKE BOOK

A COMPILATION OF JOKES + GAME RULES

This book is a
compilation of jokes
compiled & edited by
John Conrad

+

game rules, and
scoring pages
created by
John Conrad

Special thanks to freepik.com for use of the trophy silouhette on the cover.

Whatever you do...
don't laugh.

Try Not to Laugh Out Loud Challenge!

Rules & Instructions for the games

2 Player game

- sit down and face your opponent
- <u>take turns</u> reading a joke from this book
- if your opponent laughs you **score a point**!
- first one to reach **5 points** is the winner

4 Player game (Tag Team!)

- split up into teams: **Team 1 vs. Team 2**
- <u>one person</u> from each team faces off
  & takes a turn reading a joke
- if your opponent laughs **you score a point**!
- you may **tag your teamate** after any round
  to switch positions
- you are eliminated if you get **5 points.**
- if you and your teammate are both
  eliminated then your team loses.

- Last team standing wins!

Have fun & don't laugh!

How do you throw birthday party in outer space? **You planet.**

Did you hear about the lady who lost the right side of her body? **She's all-right now.**

Why was the raccoon lying in the middle of the street? **He got tired.**

Why don't they don't allow gambling during a safari? **Too many Cheetahs.**

Why don't we switch from pounds to kilograms overnight? **Because there would be mass confusion**

Want to hear a joke about a piece of paper? **Nevermind, it's tearable.**

Did you hear about the restaurant on mars? **Great food but the atmosphere is horrible.**

How many cherries grow on a cherry tree? **All of them.**

How does an eskimo build a house? **Igloos it together.**

Why did the goldfish think they were fighting a war? **They were inside a tank.**

What is the name of a man with no legs and no arms in a swimming pool? **Bob**

What is the name of a man who can't stand? **Neil**

Have you heard of the band called 678 megabtes? **If you haven't, that's okay, they haven't had a gig yet.**

Why did the rooster croos the road? **To prove it wasn't a chicken.**

Why did the golfer wear two pairs of pants? **In case he got a hole in one.**

What did the mother horse say to the baby horse? **It's past-ure bedtime.**

What do you call a horse that lives in the house next to you?
A neeeeeeigh-bor.

Why isn't the english teacher friends with every single letter of the alphabet? **She doesn't know 'Y.'**

Why can't a mountain bike stand on it's own? **It's two tired.**

What happened when the brunette got her hair bleached? **She got light-headed.**

What did the ocean do when it saw the beach? **It waved.**

What does a watch do when it's hungry? **It goes back for seconds.**

Why can't towels and wash rags tell jokes? **They have a dry sense of humor.**

What do you call a cow who can't stand up straight? **Lean beef.**

What do you call a cow without it's legs? **Ground beef.**

Why did the teacher become cross-eyed? **He could't control his pupils.**

Why did the clown retire after a bad juggling accident? **He didn't have the balls to do it anymore.**

Why isn't the runner afraid of hurdles anymore? **He got over it.**

Why didn't the hyena win the race? **It was racing a cheetah.**

Why did the tomatoe turn red? **Because it saw the salad dressing.**

Why don't vampires eat meat? **They don't like steaks.**

Why did the poster go to jail even though it was innocent? **It was framed.**

What do you call a bear with no teeth? **A gummy bear.**

Did you know they finally made a movie about clocks? **It's about time.**

How do you know someone isn't ad-dicted to brake fluid? **They can stop whenever they want.**

What should you do if you have a fear of elevators? **Take steps to avoid them.**

What did the buffalo say to his son when he left? **Bison**

Why can't you trust elevators? **They're always up to something.**

Why did the Energizer bunny get arrested? **It was charged with battery.**

Why did the skeleton go to the movie along? **He didn't have any-body to go with.**

Why didn't the skeleton ask the lady on a date? **He didn't have any guts.**

How did the lady feel when metal objects stopped shocking her when she touched them? **Ec-static.**

Why did the muffler stop working? **It was exhausted.**

Did you hear about the circus fire? **It was in-tents.**

Why did a hiker pack a phone? **In case nature called.**

Why was the father called a hero when he wouldn't let his son sleep in the middle of the day? **He prevented a kidnapping.**

Which languange in the world is spoken less than any other? **Sign language**

Did you hear about the nacho joke? **Nevermind, it's too cheesy.**

Why can't you trust atoms? **They make up everything.**

Did you hear about the dinosaur hip-hop artist? **He was a famous raptor.**

Why did the astronaut break up with his girlfriend? **He needed some space.**

What do you give a sick bird? **Tweetment**

Why don't oysters share it's belongings? **Because their shellfish.**

What do you call fake noodles? **Impastas!**

Why was the rasberry crying? **Because it's friends were in a jam.**

How do chickens get someone to do something for them? **They egg them on.**

What do you call a belt with a watch on it? **A waist of time.**

Why shouldn't you sketch with a broken drawing pencil? **It's pointless.**

What do you call a bear when there is not one bee is around? **Ears.**

What did the judge say when someone farted? **Odor in the court!**

How do you defend yourself from a queen bee? **With a B B gun.**

Did you hear about the 4 thiefs that stole a calendar? **They each got 3 months.**

What did the tomato say to the hot dog? **I'll catchup to you.**

What do you call food that isn't yours? **Nachos!**

Why did the traffic lights turn red? **It changed in the middle of the intersection.**

What did the blanket say when the maid ripped it off the bed?
I thought you had me covered.

Why didn't the lifeguard save the drowning hippy? **He was too far out man!**

Why did a baker open a bakery? **To make some dough.**

What do you call a rattlesnake who can't rattle? **A reptile dysfunction.**

How many people live in Brazil? **A brazilian.**

How do you know you were attacked by a vampire snowman? **You have frostbite.**

What happened when a frog parked his car illegally? **It got toad.**

What do you call a person who never farts in public? **A private tutor.**

What is a vampires favorite drink? **A bloody mary.**

What is a vampire's favorite dog? **A blood hound.**

Why did the science teacher stop telling jokes in class? **He didn' get a reaction.**

Why did the cookie cry? **Because his father was a wafer so long!**

Why should you never go to a seafood disco? **You could pull a mussel.**

Do you know where you can get chicken broth in bulk? **The stock market.**

Why did the octopus beat the shark in a fight? **Because it was well armed.**

How much does a hipster weigh?
An instagram.

What did daddy spider say to baby spider? **You spend too much time on the web.**

What is atheism? **It's a non-prophet organization.**

Did you hear about the brand new broom they invented? **It's sweeping the nation.**

What cheese can never be yours? **Nacho cheese.**

What did the Buffalo say to his little boy when he dropped him off at school? **Bison.**

Have you ever heard of a music group called Cellophane? **They mostly wrap.**

How was Rome split in two? **With a pair of Ceasars.**

What is a shovel? **It's a ground breaking invention.**

What did the Buddhist say when it walked up to a hot dog stand? **Make me one with everything.**

What do you call a girl with one leg that's shorter than the other? **Ilene.**

Did you hear about the theatrical performance about puns? **It was a play on words.**

Do you know sign language?
You should learn it, it's pretty handy.

Why was one banana attracted to the other? **Because she was appealing.**

Did you read the book about anti-gravity? **I couldn't put it down.**

What should you do if you are cold?
Stand in the corner. **It's 90 degrees.**

How does Moses make coffee?
Hebrews it.

What did the alien say to the pitcher
of water? **Take me to your liter.**

Did you hear about the soldier who sur-
vived mustard gas and pepper spray?
He was a seasoned veteran.

Did you read the book about glue?
I couldn't put it down.

Why shouldn't you trust atoms?
They make up everything.

What's it called when you have too
many aliens? **Extraterrestrials.**

What do cows tell each other at bedtime? **Dairy tales.**

Why didn't the lion win the race?
Because he was racing a cheetah.

What's it called when you put a cow in a
hot air balloon? **Raising the steaks.**

What kind of car does a sheep drive?
Their SuBAHHru.

Why don't vampires go to barbecues?
They don't like steaks.

How do trees access the internet?
They log on.

Why should you never trust a train?
They have loco motives.

Did you see the ad for burial plots in today's newspaper? **It's the last thing I need.**

Have you ever tried fixing a clock? **It's very time consuming.**

Why can't bicycles stand up on their own? **They are 2 tired.**

What would happen if the alarm clocks hit you back in the morning? **It would be truly alarming.**

Why is a skeleton a bad liar? **You can see right through it.**

What do you receive when you ask a lemon for help? **Lemonaid.**

A man sued an airline after it lost his luggage. **Sadly, he lost his case.**

What does a dog say when he sits down on a piece of sandpaper? **Ruff!**

100 Did you hear about my trip to the dentist? **Let me fill you in.**

Did you hear about the cartoonist that was found dead in his home? **The details are sketchy.**

Did you know that the old woman who lived in a shoe wasn't the sole owner? **Strings were attached.**

Did you hear about the crime in the parking garage? **It was wrong on so many levels.**

Did you hear about the new meal they serve on the flight? **It's a bit plane.**

Have you ever tried to milk a cow which has been cut in half? **It's Udder madness.**

Why are there fences on graveyards? **Because people are dying to get in.**

Why do trees have so many friends? **They branch out.**

Why should you never discuss infinity with a mathematician? **They can go on about it forever.**

Why don't some couples go to the gym? **Because some relationships don't work out.**

Why shouldn't you trust people that do acupuncture? **They're a bunch of back stabbers.**

What did the lady say when her persistent banker wouldn't stop talking to her? **Just leave me a loan!**

Did you know I ordered a book of puns yesterday? **I didn't get it.**

Did you know that my friends say i look better without glasses? **I just can't see it.**

Do you know why you shouldn't judge chicken broth by the way it looks? **It's very soup-erficial.**

Did you know I changed my smartphone name to the Titanic? **It's syncing now.**

Did you hear that Jill broke her finger on her right hand today? **On the other hand she was completely fine.**

Did you know I got hit in the head with a can of soda? **Luckily it was a soft drink.** 35

Why isn't suntanning an Olympic sport?
Because the best you can ever get is bronze.

What do you mean June is over?
I'm Julying.

Why did the candle quit his job?
Because he felt burned out.

Did you hear about the construction worker that lost his legs on the job?
He's now just a handyman.

Did you know I tried going to bed with music?
It gave me sound sleep.

Did you hear about the aliens that landed? **They were down to earth.**

Why did the smart phone have to wear glasses? **It lost its contacts.**

How do mountains see? **They peak.**

Why do novice pirates make terrible singers? **Because they can't hit the high seas.**

Did you hear about the two peanuts that were walking in a tough neighborhood? **One of them was a-salted.**

Did you hear about the two ropes were walking in a tough neighborhood? **One of them was a-frayed.**

What kind of shoes do ninjas wear? **Sneakers.**

Did you know I got a master's degree in being ignored? **No one seems to care.**

What did the sea monster say after eating the ship? **I can't believe I ate the hull thing.**

Why can't storks carry big babies? **They're too heavy, they need a crane.**

What happened when the bartender broke up with her boyfriend? **He asked for another shot.**

What happened when he couldn't fix the washing machine? **He threw in the towel.**

Why does the man want to buy nine rackets? **Cause tennis too many.**

Why don't cannibals eat clowns? **Because they taste funny.**

Why did the cook make a lot of pasta? **Because he got paid in lots of Pennes.**

39

Did you hear about the doctor that broke his leg while auditioning for a local play? **He still made the cast.**

Did you hear about the tale of the haunted refrigerator? **It was chilling.**

Why are frogs so happy? **They eat whatever bugs them.**

Did you hear about the new wooden whistle I bought? **It wooden whistle.**

What did the mummy do when it was sore? **It went to a Cairo-practor.**

Don't you feel sorry for shopping carts? **They're always getting pushed around.**

Why did they close down the still-life art exhibit? **It was not moving at all.**

Why should you never make pig puns? **They are so boaring.**

What do you do when balloons are hurt? **You helium.**

What did one hat says to the other? **You stay here, I'll go on a-head.**

How many tickles does it take to make an octopus laugh? **Ten-tickles.**

When does a farmer dance? **When he drops the beets.**

What did the scientist do when he wanted to clone a deer? **He bought a doe it yourself kit.**

How many puns have they made in Germany? **Nein**

Did you hear about the invention of the white board? **It was remarkable.**

Can February March? **No, but April May.**

Why do people hate Russian Dolls? **They are so full of themselves.**

What do you do to an open wardrobe? **You closet.**

Why did the magazine about ceiling fans go out of business? **Because of low circulation.**

Did you hear about the aquatic mammals that escaped the zoo? **It was otter chaos.**

Why do lumberjacks love computers? **They enjoy logging in.**

Why do garbage collectors drive big slow trucks? **Because they are rubbish drivers.**

What happened to the church when it relocated? **It had an organ transplant.**

Why did the scarecrow get promoted? **He was outstanding in his field.**

What do prisoners use to call each other? **Cell phones.**

What does a clock do when it's hungry? **It goes back four seconds.**

You know why I like egg puns? **They crack me up!**

Want to hear a pun about ghosts? **That's the spirit!**

Did you know I make clown shoes? **It's no small feat.**

Did you hear about the circus that caught on fire? **It was in tents.**

What is the one day of the week that eggs are afraid of?
Fry-day.

Why was the hen mad at the farmer?
He beat the eggs.

Why shouldn't more than one dishwasher wash dishes? **It's hard for them to stay in sink.**

What do people who use umbrellas have in common? **They are all under the weather.**

What planet is like a circus? **Saturn, it has three rings!**

Why did the lion eat the tightrope walker?

He wanted a well-balanced meal!

What's the name of the locksmith with a lisp? **Keith**

Did you know that dogs can't get MRI's? **Apparently, catscan**

What do you call a camel with no humps? **Humphrey**

Why do all hot dogs look alike?
They're inbred

Why didn't the lifeguard save the drowning hippy? **He was too far out man**

Did you hear about the kidnapping at school? **He was napping**

What do you call a person with no body and no nose? **Nobody nose.**

What do you call a bear with no teeth? **A gummy bear.**

Score Pages

The following **score pages** are to help you keep track of score. There are scoresheets for **2-player** and **4-player games.**

To keep score

Write the name down for each player. Color, cross-out, or fill-in, one face each turn that your opponent laughs. First player will all faces colored, crossed-out, or filled-in, loses! See rules for 2-player and 4-player games at the beginning of this book.

Tips

Place a bookmark or sticky note on the scoreard you are using so you don't lose your place. Cut-out or tear out the pages if necessary. Also, you can photocopy the scorecards so you don't run out.

2-Player Score Page

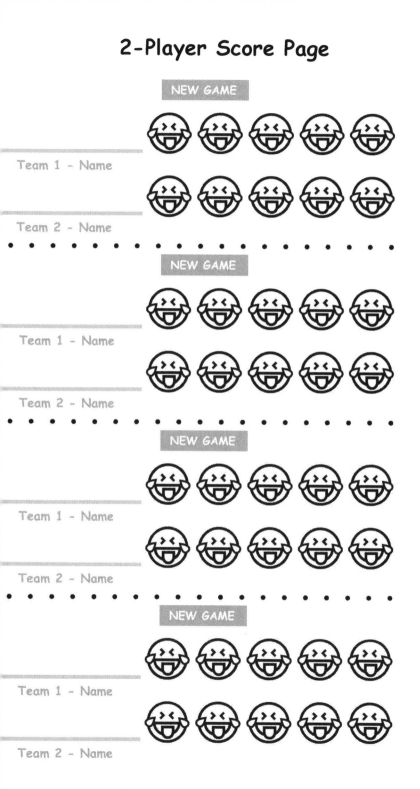

2-Player Score Page

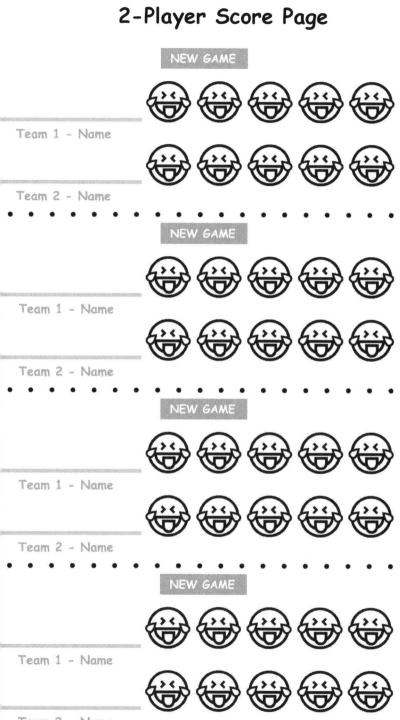

NEW GAME

Team 1 - Name

Team 2 - Name

NEW GAME

Team 1 - Name

Team 2 - Name

NEW GAME

Team 1 - Name

Team 2 - Name

NEW GAME

Team 1 - Name

Team 2 - Name

2-Player Score Page

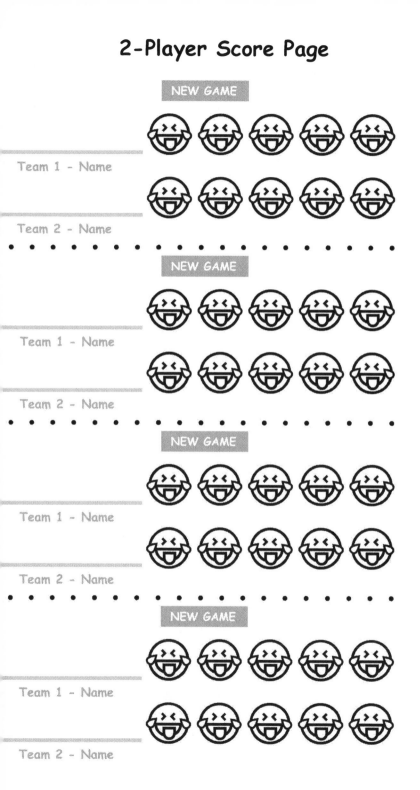

NEW GAME

Team 1 - Name

Team 2 - Name

NEW GAME

Team 1 - Name

Team 2 - Name

NEW GAME

Team 1 - Name

Team 2 - Name

NEW GAME

Team 1 - Name

Team 2 - Name

2-Player Score Page

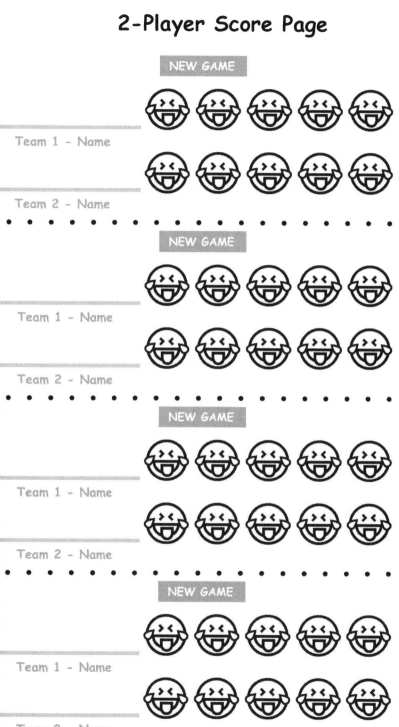

NEW GAME

Team 1 - Name

Team 2 - Name

NEW GAME

Team 1 - Name

Team 2 - Name

NEW GAME

Team 1 - Name

Team 2 - Name

NEW GAME

Team 1 - Name

Team 2 - Name

2-Player Score Page

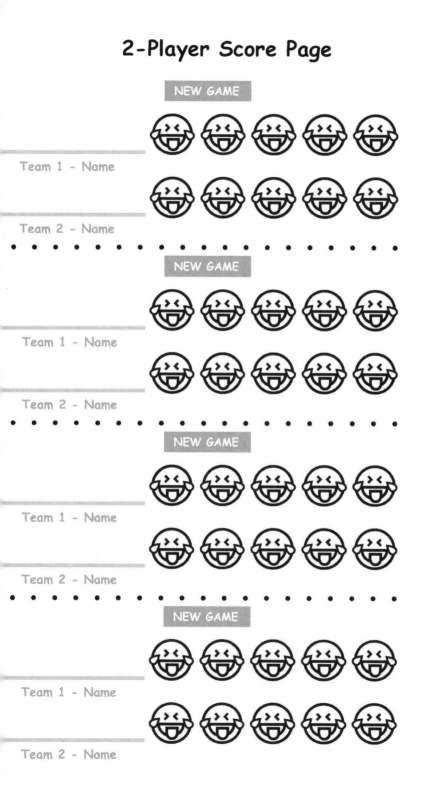

NEW GAME

Team 1 - Name

Team 2 - Name

NEW GAME

Team 1 - Name

Team 2 - Name

NEW GAME

Team 1 - Name

Team 2 - Name

NEW GAME

Team 1 - Name

Team 2 - Name

2-Player Score Page

NEW GAME

Team 1 - Name

Team 2 - Name

NEW GAME

Team 1 - Name

Team 2 - Name

NEW GAME

Team 1 - Name

Team 2 - Name

NEW GAME

Team 1 - Name

Team 2 - Name

2-Player Score Page

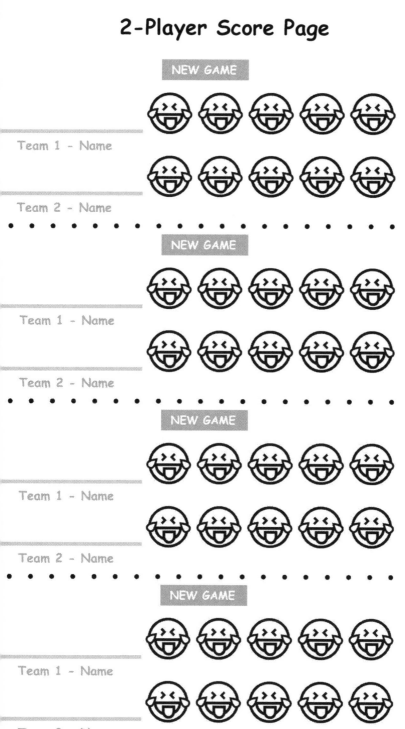

NEW GAME

Team 1 - Name

Team 2 - Name

NEW GAME

Team 1 - Name

Team 2 - Name

NEW GAME

Team 1 - Name

Team 2 - Name

NEW GAME

Team 1 - Name

Team 2 - Name

4-Player Score Page

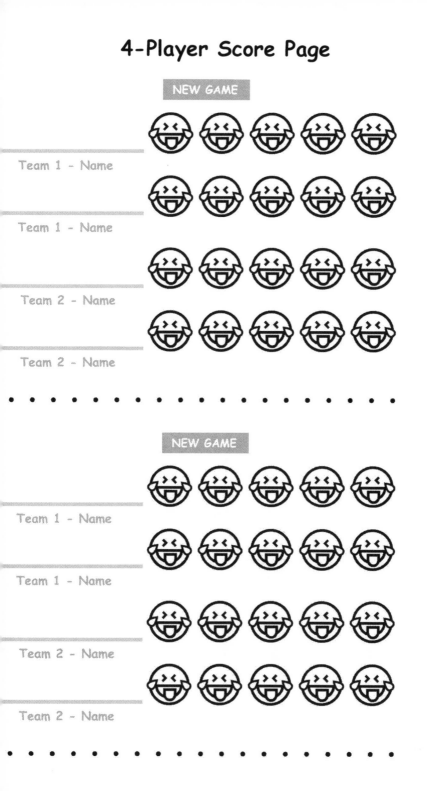

NEW GAME

Team 1 - Name

Team 1 - Name

Team 2 - Name

Team 2 - Name

NEW GAME

Team 1 - Name

Team 1 - Name

Team 2 - Name

Team 2 - Name

4-Player Score Page

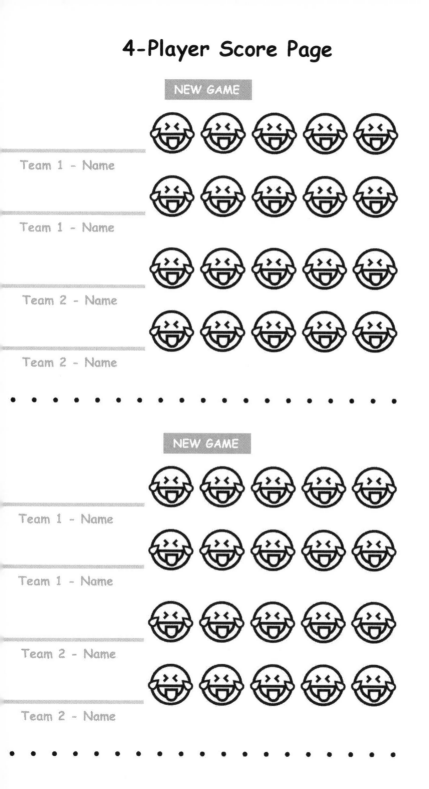

4-Player Score Page

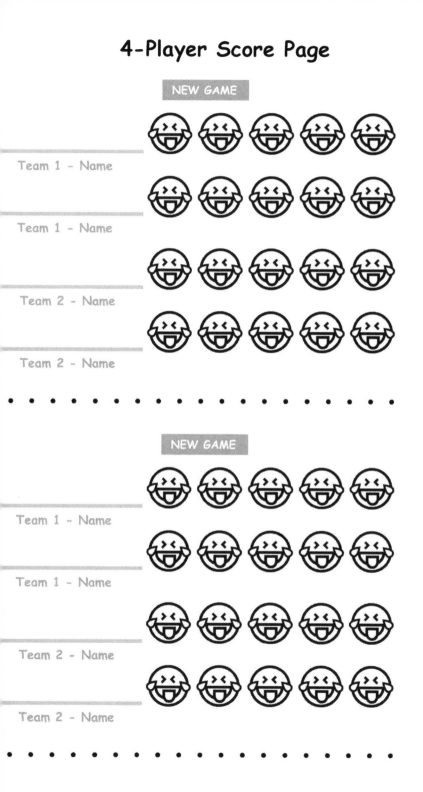

Team 1 - Name

Team 1 - Name

Team 2 - Name

Team 2 - Name

Team 1 - Name

Team 1 - Name

Team 2 - Name

Team 2 - Name

4-Player Score Page

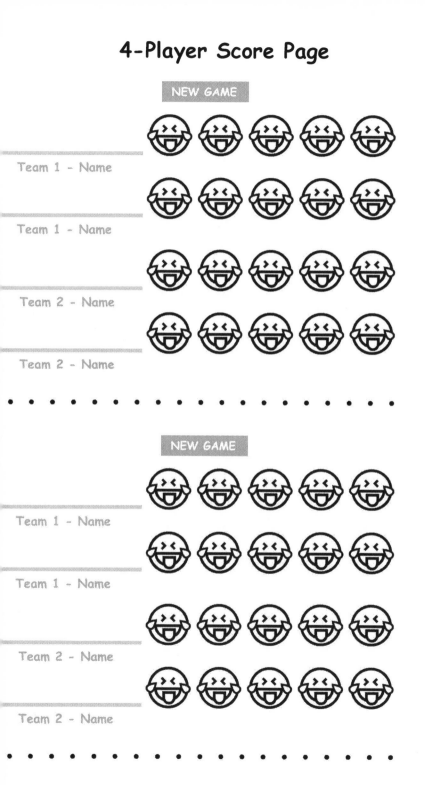

4-Player Score Page

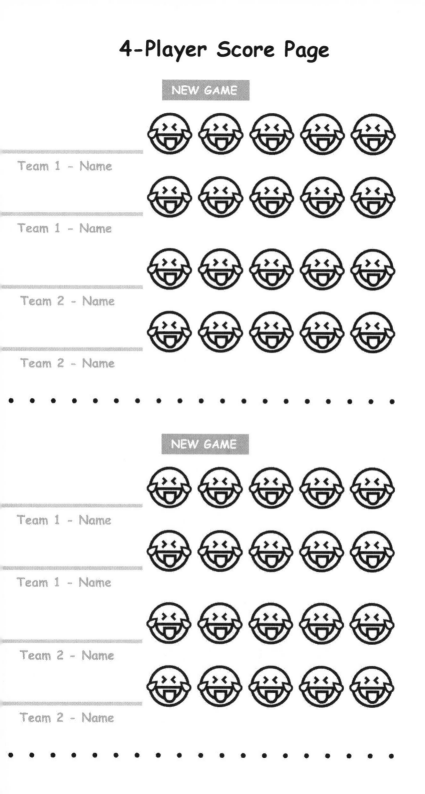

4-Player Score Page

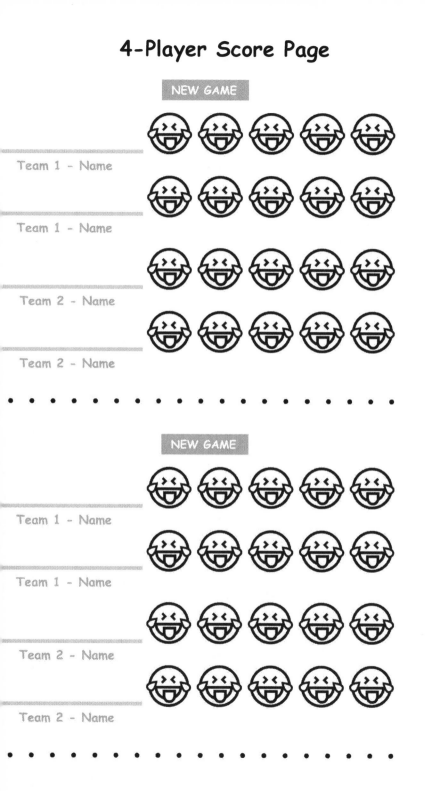

NEW GAME

Team 1 - Name

Team 1 - Name

Team 2 - Name

Team 2 - Name

NEW GAME

Team 1 - Name

Team 1 - Name

Team 2 - Name

Team 2 - Name

Made in the USA
Monee, IL
10 May 2023